Teacher, I Honor You
Poems honoring young people, parents and teachers

poems by

Helene McGlauflin

Finishing Line Press
Georgetown, Kentucky

Teacher, I Honor You
Poems honoring young people, parents and teachers

This book is dedicated to parents and teachers everywhere who devote their time, talent, energy and sometimes, their entire lives, to our young people.

It is written to honor our young people, who struggle, learn and grow with the help of adults who care.

Copyright © 2016 by Helene McGlauflin
ISBN 978-1-944899-14-1 First Edition
All rights reserved under International and Pan-American Copyright Conventions. No part of this book may be reproduced in any manner whatsoever without written permission from the publisher, except in the case of brief quotations embodied in critical articles and reviews.

ACKNOWLEDGMENTS

I thank the *The Goose River Anthology 2012* for first publishing *Mother's Day Without You* and *December Birth* and The Topsham Public Library for giving *Root Cellar* honorable mention in its *Joy of Pen* competition, 2014.

I thank my children, Molly and Conor, who have allowed me the privilege of being a mother, have been my muses, and enriched my life in thousands of ways. I thank my daughter Molly and her husband Sam for bringing Mabel into the world, my granddaughter. I thank my husband Bruce for supporting my journey in every way.

I thank all the students I have known in my 30 year career as an educator who have taught me more about myself, about the art of teaching, learning and life, than I can ever express. I thank the many educators I have known who have inspired this collection, especially the staff at the Woodside Elementary School in Topsham, Maine, my muses for so many years. Many of the poems in this collection were first written and read for my colleagues to honor the last day of school.

Editor: Christen Kincaid

Cover Art: Lonie Laffley Ellis

Author Photo: Rose Nelson

Cover Design: Elizabeth Maines

Printed in the USA on acid-free paper.
Order online: www.finishinglinepress.com
    also available on amazon.com

Author inquiries and mail orders:
Finishing Line Press
P. O. Box 1626
Georgetown, Kentucky 40324
U. S. A.

Table of Contents

Honoring Young People

Born 1
Watching you 2
A Young Writer Speaks 3
Portraits of Young People at the Basketball Game 4
If Only, But Then 5
Studying Mary Cassatt's "Child in a Straw Hat" 7
Artists of Tomorrow at Bowdoin College 8
Promise 9
December Birth 10

Honoring Parents

Standing in Rain 11
Girl at the Pool 12
Night Watch 13
A Bicycle for Molly 15
Begin 16
Just One Pint 17
My Mother's Hands 18
Mother's Day Without You 20
Root Cellar 22

Honoring Teachers

A Letter from Society to Our Nation's Teachers 23
A Letter to Society from its Teachers: a reply 25
The Perfect School 27
Forgive Everything 28
The Enormous No 30
Teacher, I Honor You 32
No Child Left Behind 2005 34
The Master Teacher 35
A Single Star 36
Retiring Haiku 37

Honoring Young People

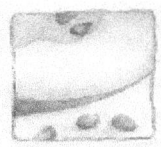

Born

On the day you were born
angels sang, a great spirit
entered with your first breath
and will never leave you.
It was right to cry

Watching You

There is nothing so pure
as this: you, just hours old
peeking at me through slitted eyes
not sure about opening to here
from there. Skin untouched by sun
wind, water, cloth; rosebud mouth
and tongue groping to find

There is nothing so new
as this: your face practicing, eyebrows
rise and fall, a maybe smile then a scrunch
hint of frown, yawn, yelp, not yet
happiness, defiance, boredom or sorrow,
lips smacking that will one day kiss
tiny twitches too unsteady to express

There is nothing but wonder here
between the worlds, your presence
an embodiment of a particular peacefulness
it will later take hundreds of hours of meditation
to reclaim, stillness exuding from every cell,
secrets from another world revealed in the
shy opening of those eyes,
in that moment before lids close.

A Young Writer Speaks

My teacher has told me
to be at my desk and write,
"be your own boss" she says
but I don't know what to write!
The poems inside me are not
like poems in books:
my poems are soft, like spring rain
funny but maybe only I will laugh
so fierce they are crazy tornadoes
so ordinary who will read them?

How can I write a poem?
All I have are
my eyes seeing white light or rainbows
my ears hearing music or cacophony
my skin feeling a pleasure or a pinch
my tongue tasting sweet or sour
my nose smelling flowers or trash
my heart beating or bleeding

But my poems
the secret ones inside me not written or
the ones on a page, are mine. Billions of
people walk the earth daily; no one else
saw, heard, felt, tasted, smelled something
the way I have, no one will chose that word
but me. My poems: I hold them, imagine them,
write them, speak them

Portraits of Young People
At the Basketball Game

Young men muscular and glistening
with sweat dripping, followed by mop,
some are large, lumbering down court
others lithe with finesse, sporting bodies
to hot–dogged crowds

Costumed young women cheering as they
flash perfect teeth, flip bouncing blonde curls
exposing breasts, bellies, hips, buttocks with
luring looks like sirens, so suggestive it
warrants rating

Referee fit and serious, whistle-ready
with hair pulled plainly into tail, back
straight, an amazon unmoved by
booing arrows ricocheting off
the shield of her striped strength

Little ones run up, down bleachers
boys yelling freely and sweaty from pushing
girls with messy pony tails and breast buds
bouncing under tee shirts watching the crowd,
watching the game, making up their minds

If Only, But Then

If only you had been cherished enough, not fallen
from that third story window onto arms of concrete
leaving you forever in the now………..but then
you would not look with newness on this day,
challenge a hubris about past, future

If only your chromosomes had not misbehaved in
utero, baffling your genetic makeup irrevocably…..
but then you would not have made walking
an achievement at nine or offered an
unhappy world your abiding smile

If only you had taken your first breath at birth
not paused for those crucial brain-starving seconds
leaving your limbs spastic, speech labored………….
but then you would not embody righteous frustration
nor teach the able bodied the dignity of struggle

If only something had not gone awry in the amygdala
calling you to turn for satisfaction to a compelling
inner world with a private passcode……………………..
but then who defines normal, who really knows what
it means to connect, who ever shares their passcode?

If only every human vice had not been showered over
you continually since birth skewing your perceptions
of sincerity and love…………………………………..
but then you might not reveal the nature of raw
honesty, spirited resistance, angry strength

If only we could grasp the stars, our cousins
sharing our essence from light years, so close and
like us at times, so remote and distant at others.......
but then we might be tricked into believing we are
significant, with out clumsy feet barely touching ground
regularly inattentive to traces of light

Studying Mary Cassatt's Child in a Straw Hat

Did Mary know she had captured
that kind of child, the little sad ones
who haunt your dreams, their pale faces
your only audience when you step onto a
weathered soapbox that holds no weight?

You stand before her, dream of taking her home
and find you want to sing a song of the sad ones,
make it a lament:
the ones so thirsty one tiny drop of kindness
will be returned with geyser gushing love,
their adoration so intense it brings you to your knees
wishing from the bottom of some pit you could be god.
The ones so harmed they spit suspiciously when
your kindness hits their tongues, taste buds ruined
by souring, protectively rejecting any promise of sweetness.
The ones so dispirited they no longer recognize drops
of any kind, stare blankly at you from a shroud of disbelief.

As the art holds you in the good company of song
your heart inexplicably lightens as your glance moves
from face to the untattered hat, the clean pinafore, the
chubby torso, allowing your next stanza to spring up
an octave, in hope for a future allegro

Artists of Tomorrow at Bowdoin College

These young people are well groomed:
straight smiles, gowns sparkling, suits pressed
the ones sitting near me in audience smell of
soap and privilege, the innocent kind that has
not yet reflected on where the stork dropped
them or their distance from the unwashed

They come to play for us in summer
their youth evident in their smooth skin,
shining dark hair and laughter between sets
but as they step on the stage, all is serious.
That first gesture of tuning contains the thousand
hours of practice and sacrifice: the early awkward
notes, the expected tears, smiles, nagging, pride
that brought them to this moment, poised to perform

They begin always with perfect synchronized precision
notes so pure they pierce the heart like a scalpel,
opening the audience to receive the tenderness
of this art that can only be expressed truly tonight
by these, our young. All this held by a sacred silence
they honor before the first note, after the last

Promise
For Molly and Sam
on your wedding day

Join hands at this crossroad
walk gingerly into your sunrise, feel the
new road beneath your four feet, your width
side by side, the combustion in your clasp

Keep walking, soon it will be morning:
as the sun begins to dry dew, breathe
in the freshness of your new day, try to
identify that fragrance, your future

Pause at noon, look behind, ahead
smile at one another, join hands again that
inevitably parted for what was required, find
satisfaction in the work of your morning

Stroll into the afternoon, help each other
when it becomes very warm and shadows
fall in surprising places. Now is the time to
dip into the reservoir of your companionship

Find a lamp that can be lit together at dusk
when one of your innumerable days is done
may sunset remind you of everything precious,
like the power and fragility of love

When night comes, let the darkness teach you
of your collective courage, your width as a couple
your steely strength as two, your shared road.
Hold hands facing east, look for light, never let go.

December Birth

What is this birth
so many wait for as
darkness and cold
bring us to our knees,
that story of a girl
homeless, blessed
laboring in straw
warmed by beasts
while angels sang
shepherds feared
and kings followed
that star compelling
each to an irresistible
newness?
Even now who can
explain the comfort
of waking after solstice
surrounded, still, by
darkness but changed
by a simple certainty:
light

Honoring Parents

Standing in Rain

He held an accusing sign
wore a wide brimmed hat
bolo tie, complacent grin
and stood in pouring rain,
stayed as I went across
and back over the bridge

He began like each of us, a small
seed with tail swimming blindly
to what life longed for, a lucky one
among millions that found
a home in an egg, a place in a uterus,
stayed long enough to evolve

Murder, an opinion like cement
that can never dry or cast in rain,
a decision he would never face,
his protruding belly forever empty
of a small life that would need
complicated tending for a lifetime

Rain
pour over us as we try to stand
be the seeds of men spilling into wombs
be the tears of women conceiving with
or without love, with or without consent
be the first wet cry of babies wanted, babies
unwanted, babies awaited with ambivalence
then cleanse us as you course down streams,
bless us as you converge with rivers,
receive us as you flow into the loving,
briny arms of our oceans

The Girl at the Pool

She looks fourteen
pierced lip, tattoos cascading
colorfully down one arm, bikini
outlining a perfect protruding belly:
unapologetically bold, abundantly due.
Her freckled face reveals an innocent
ignorance: youth unable to grasp
the magnitude of her weight, the gravity
of a casual conception, this life that could
not help itself and will grow, force its way out
and demand so much of her, more than she
may have. How can she know?

Night Watch

I am not alone

There is the night
keeping close about me
holding the tired, the ill,
the wakeful, the anguished
with maddening equanimity

There is my son
sleeping after restlessness,
eyelids mercifully covering an
empty fevered gaze. His breath
steady, his cheeks tender

There are children
forever fevering, calling from
strange dreams, crying for water,
waking after health's triumph,
oblivious to fever's cost

There are mothers
forever tending ill children who have
lived and died despite broth, prayer.
Their arms hold instinctive respect,
rock with the patience of the powerless

There is death
fever's now-distant cousin,
claiming his familial rights
to be here, to hover near, to
whisper, "not him, not now"

There is love
startled awake by death
fretting and fussing maternally,
embracing fear in her fathomless body
ready for any vigil at any time

A Bicycle for Molly

I had a first bicycle when I was nine
new and royal blue. The seat was
a white banana, handlebars so shiny
they caught the sun on bright days
they curved up, turned out like lilies with
grips that held long multi-colored tassels
that clicked and fluttered endlessly until
I braided them one day.

Blue was my stallion
I rode with the wind, knew passion as
it whirled within my shirt, I would ride
hard up the hugest hill, come down
without braking, even around the bend.
Courage! and love, for I spent hours on Blue,
hours dreaming of riding while biding time
doing the things girls do.

But the rains came and my mother forgot,
or never knew about bicycles and
all that can happen to the shine, so
                              I left it out.
The chrome dulled, the chain slacked,
I grew to forget what I knew but if I had
only known about sheds I might still have
Old Blue to give my Molly at nine

Begin

You have packed your favorite mug
the one just a few inches high and wide
that looked newly turned, quickly glazed,
just removed from the kiln, purposely
imperfect with bumpy impressions of the
creator's fingertips.
The single word BEGIN called from one side
written in an old typewriter font so authentic
it startled the imagination into hearing
the distinctive zip paper made when pulled
from the platen in satisfaction or despair

How do I know it will haunt me when you go?
It was that careless toss into your kitchen box,
dear frangible gesture! It is that poignant word
so real now as you obey its command, that
challenge posed by cup's artistic nonchalance:
the unconscious urgency of the verb, the small
handle able to hold just the single finger of a man,
the infuriating way it was always showing up
in past tense around the house, coffee slick on
side, insisting to be washed and so brought
back to present tense again

The station wagon is heavy now as you
drive out of sight, full of the boxes you know
and those I stashed secretly for strangers marked
"keep upright" and "irregular, handle with care."
Listen for the empty one whispering the word *begin*,
        which has always been,
           is, the only word

Just One Pint
> *on St. Patrick's Day*

Order a pint tonight, watch as the bartender
skillfully tips the glass just so, fills it with
creamy tan foam, settles it on drain. The froth
coats the sides lovingly, the peaty ale displaces
foam so slowly you might die of thirst waiting
but the moment always arrives to drink, feel its
creamy texture caress the back of the throat,
and know it is good for you

But have just one pint tonight
not many, not every day, not for a lifetime
for while you sing there are children waiting for
you at home, worried about your whereabouts
awaiting the consequences of your condition.
Their incredulous hearts have been broken
seeing that in the competition for affection
the pint wins

And if you can have just one, especially
if your blood stirs with the Guinness and
your marrow recognizes the lure, be proud
tonight you have broken a chain, stood
bravely and caught the hand of a scourge
that has enslaved your ancestors for centuries.
Now is the time to sing, with your sweet tenor
voice, so the children might sleep

My Mother's Hands

When I reach for her now
all I touch is my mother's hands.
Her face frozen in pictures, her voice
silent as in her life, yet her hands vivid
those many hours I watched them
indelible threads sewn from eyes, to mind,
to heart, pulled taut then knotted at my core

Fingers so slim, rings so tiny,
I marveled as I held them at her death
a petite woman that bore me, four others
a mountain of anguish and barrels of grief
whose slender hands held babies, fabric
and cigarettes adeptly but could never quite
hold the true Theresa.

I envied her nails.
Slender with what seemed the perfect curve
mine lacked, the cuticles and nails never bitten,
Emory board always ready for repair. She only
used clear *Hard as Nails* for polish, dabbing it
onto my shabby bitten ones so I would stop,
but how could I when this clear coating was all
she had and had to give?

Many hours I watched her hands smooth cloth before cutting, catch a few threads with needle to hem, wet a thread end to allow that tricky stiff slide into eye. During her decline I one day watched an admittedly deranged, strangely elegant dance of her sewing hands. Sitting up in her hospital bed, she gracefully, repeatedly took an imaginary thread, placed it on lips to moisten, threaded it through the eye of all needles, knotted it convincingly with care. Her hands then rhythmically arched and pierced what I will always hope was exceptionally fine blue satin patterned with clouds, hers, and hers alone to stitch for all eternity

Mother's Day without You

We have shared a hundred million moments
missed millions of moments since,
will miss a billion moments more

Mysteries of my womb
remember me sometimes, won't you
when you see a newborn, find a lullaby hidden
in a sweet secret place I tucked in long ago,
when you sew a button on a shirt with ease
cook a meal, go to bed early, or feel yourself
planted firmly on earth, instinctively sensing only
hurricane force could knock you down, when
you give love, see love, find love, know love
                then I will know
                our shared moments mattered

Think of me sometimes, won't you,
when you crave, pour, then savor a cup of tea
plant a marigold seed in a small cup, smile seeing
bluets shivering as breeze passes through grass in May
climb a mountain and during that final push to summit
feel the heart that once shared a cadence with mine
beating hard with the affirmation: alive, alive, alive
or look at stars, know them as yourself continually
shining for light years though surrounded by black space
                then I will know
                there are millions less one I have missed

Call me sometimes, won't you
when I can still offer something you need or you
want to share with the certainty I will care,
if ever you feel unloved, abandoned or afraid and seek
the comfort of an old sweater, a poached egg, an ocean breeze
when you have time for a meandering conversation that strolls
in a place so familiar it recurs in a dream, or on the day
you know a loneliness deep in your core creating an inexplicable
yearning only a long known voice can soothe
                      then there will be
                      billions less one we will share

Root Cellar

The smell of soil reaches you first as you descend,
face brushed by cobwebs, hand steadied on rail
even the musty darkness is a comfort in this
place dug by the strong, committed to
staving off starvation in a womb of earth. You keep
cheery company here with carrots, turnips, potatoes
pickles and in one corner, mason jars of light

You remember storing them that high summer day
when the sun shone without interruption on water
scattering small petals of light over the surface,
twinklings multiplying the longer you looked, your
face welcoming a certain warm blush. Breathing in
you filled, then covered all the inner jars you could,
sealing in this living luminosity
reassured it could be stored for those dark days before
solstice when every cell is keening over the loss of light

Moth-drawn to corner you take jar in hand, eager for the pop
of broken seal, lift rim to mouth, pour the precious preserves
down, in, coursing through every vein until each cell is lit
with a confidence that as cold and despair lurk outside, you
will never starve if you can descend, return to your store
sit in a corner among jars in the gloaming, trust the quiet,
the silent light as a promise from the root cellar

Honoring Teachers

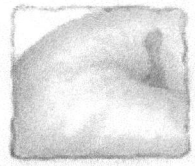

A Letter from Society to Our Nation's Teachers

Dear Teachers

We are moved to write to you today on the last day of school,
to tell you we recognize and appreciate all you do for us.
We rely on you to support our democracy by creating literate
citizens
by socializing and civilizing our young, by offering us the ambitious
hope of a free, equal education for all. Our debt to you is
immeasurable.

You know some of us, the visible ones who attend parent meetings
vote yes, send snacks and supplies, bring a gift with a thank you
and occasionally show up in high places: a governor's wife or
presidential
hopeful. We are the people who know that you are professionals,
that the work is demanding, that summer renewal is essential,
that you would never intentionally leave a child behind

There are many more of us, though, invisible ones who say little,
do not vote, and may not have stepped in your doors since we left.
But we remember you. We remember you always said good
morning,
that day you recommended a book we finally liked, that too-hard
subject you never abandoned, that look communicating belief
that we could actually go somewhere, be someone.

We are the burger king servers, the scientists, custodians
police officers, haridressers, nurses, lawyers, , computer techs,

housecleaners, librarians, artists, snow plowers, clergy, farmers homemakers, atheletes, oil deliverers, CEOs, trash collectors. From the mansions to the streets, from ocean to ocean , we are everywhere and you have known us all.

We are sorry for many things, how unsupportive we can seem when your piece of the pie is never the size of defense, roads or things we must tend. We cannot easily explain why those of us who can throw, hit, kick or dunk a ball professionally make enough in one year to employ 500 of you or buy 80 million pencils.

We hope you will accept our regrets and our possible promise that someday things may be different. Someday we hope to all be visible, vocal and wealthy enough so you would have everything you need without worry.
In this future, you would need supplies and receive them, have an idea, implement it and in tight times money would be unquestioningly reallocated
to education. There would be no more bake sales.

Until that day, we offer you our regrets, our thanks and our hope.

Sincerely, Society

A Letter to Society from Your Teachers, a reply

Dear Society:

Thank you for thinking of us. We noticed your letter
was well written, articulate, had poetic sense. We
are proud of your skills: we were there the first day
you wrote a letter, the days you hated writing ensuing letters
the day you felt a gratitude for being able to write at all.

We are replying to tell you why we teach.
The cynical among you may smile, expecting us
to say the health insurance, the summers, the schedule
but if that were the whole or the only story
there would be no truth to name, no reply required.

We care about our young citizens. It may surprise you
to hear when we seem fatigued or picket over a contract but
we want this caring to be clean: we know we are part of
something bigger than our classrooms, we know we save some,
make a difference for a few and worry about the future of the rest.

We believe in the ambition of democracy
that a literate citizenry is a worthy goal, that education
is a privilege to elect, that being free is a responsibility.
We know a terror and possibility when we hold a class
in our hands and feel the weight of equality every day.

(cont.)

We are glad you see us for our classrooms are your mirror,
a reflection of our societal successes, our embarrassing woes:
see your melting pot in the dress, color and abilities of our students
see the economic downturn in the young who are hungry, homeless
see the disparity of class in attendance and achievement
see the living dream in groomed children from supported homes,
do not turn away from the nightmare in the eyes of the forgotten

But know this: any child can walk through our doors
and have a teacher, a meal, a place, a chance.

                                                  Sincerely, Your Teachers

The Perfect School

The perfect school is possible.
As you walk through the doors you are
immediately worthy, already smart,
infinitely capable. The students arrive either
smiling, or confident they will be comforted.
They know they are here to learn, that working
hard holds dignity, that doing the right thing
is satisfying. The students regularly attend,
grow, improve and understand.

At the perfect school, the staff love young people,
smile daily, are physically and emotionally well.
They are excited about teaching, inspired by learning
can see and search for the educational spark on a young
face. They believe problems can be examined, solved
or appropriately ignored. Their patience is boundless.
They exhibit fortitude, a hardy endurance about the system,
even after years of cuts, changes and institutional folly.

The perfect school is a sun in the center of a town or city
shedding light and warmth indiscriminately on all the people
of that place, all the surrounding towns and cities, all the beings
of the state, the nation, the world and the universe. Yes,
even the stars are effected. The perfect school is here, now
inside of you, inside of me. You carry it wherever you go.

Forgive Everything

Come with me to an open field
together let us stand under the cloudless sky,
feel the warmth of sun, the happiness of summer
and hold the string of your favorite colored balloon,
filled with the helium of forgiveness

Begin by forgiving the system
For never living up to some promise
for its lunacy, its struggles, its surprises
for the times it fails you, your students, your community

Forgive the school building;
the front door that locks you out after dismissal
the temperature of your room: too hot or too cold?
the broken clocks, the crumblings, the designs

Forgive the tools you need:
the copier for breaking when you came in early to prep
computers that malfunction, supplies that dwindle
the laminating film, for being expensive

Forgive the schedule:
for changing at the last minute, being unclear,
outdated or just wrong, for never holding everything.
Can time be forgiven?

Forgive the assessments:
for being so numerous, for keeping you from teaching
for failing to tell the whole story of growth
for turning out not smarter, and comically out of balance

Forgive the substitutes, who exist or not
who fail to follow the plans it took hours to write
who leave long notes about misbehavior or no notes at all
who fail to leave a broom for all the sweeping up required

Forgive the children:
for running in the halls and starting conflicts
for failing to do homework or not liking your class
for sneezing on you or breaking your heart

Forgive the parents:
whose homes have no place for learning
who never come, always come, always forget or never forget
whose suffering is greater than their love for their children

Forgive your colleagues:
the misunderstandings, miscommunications
difficulties and frustrations , the perfectly
imperfect group process each year-forgive everything

Forgive yourself:
the one more thing you could not do for that student
your foggy mind, your tired body, your hurt feelings
your inescapable humanness

Ready? Look up at the sky, begin the count down, down
until the string slips from your fingers, watch forgiveness
lift the balloons away to vanishing. Together, let us receive the
the ease of release, the charm of this multicolored letting go

The Enormous No

No slides down the birth canal, arrives in the
cry when the betrayal is first felt: the snug
warm womb traded for its opposite. Before
speech, *No's* irascible voice can be heard like
a herald from every high chair

Like a hurricane who gains force over
the water of age, on the day the toddler
first shouts his name with satisfaction,
already he defies category. *No* is then
delusionally confident by the first day
of school that he, alone, can master the sea

When you meet *No*, he is a most
unavoidable, unwelcome guest. He shakes
hands firmly with each of us, no one is spared, so
every parent, teacher, coach, counselor, professor,
can find him at the start, middle or end
of any lesson, lecture, class or game

You have heard him, haven't you
when he states his name with entitlement or
shares his more clever mutations: I don't want to,
this is boring, you can't make me; the impassive oks
and other verbal sparing so swift you hardly notice
when your sword was lost

You have seen him, haven't you
in that tired slouch, the distracted yawn,
the downward glance at gadget, the inexplicable
laughter, the inside jokes, the defiant gesture,
the absences, substandard work, test not
checked, room not cleaned, task half completed

But the enormous *No* does not know he needs you
to see through his protective placenta to his twin,
Yes, waiting to be born. You are a roosting hen clucking
assurance or a rooster cock-a-doodly demanding
respect, until *Yes* stirs, cracks open then parts
the shell to stand on wobbly legs, peep

Teacher, I Honor You

Beyond sentimentality,
past hallmark cards with the corny clauses
helping hands, making a difference, patient and kind;
on the far side of endearing gifts: apple, candle
mug or hug; in the center of the vortex where
you know everything : who's following, who's lost,
who goes where when, who gets what when
what's fair, what's not, what's up
there, Teacher, I honor you.

I honor your commitment:
showing up each day when rested or tired,
ill or well, enthusiastic or discouraged, prepared or not;
holding up under the workload like a Hercules:
the endless materials that require finding, sorting, explaining;
assessments to create, give, grade; data to collect, examine, share;
responding to emails, inquiries, the "if you have a minutes"
and "could you justs," the constant clusters of students, staff
swarming like insatiable guppies clamoring to fed

I honor your flexibility
your gracious acceptance and skillful handling of
the daily serendipity: fire drills, sudden duties
cancelled guests, bus delays, assemblies, students
needing everything you have, bulging backpacks
portending things alive or dangerous, bodily fluids
near, next to or on you, initiatives that blow in, up
then pop
You go with the flow, making rivers look rigid
you bend and you move, making Gumby so green

I honor your sense of humor
your surprising smiles at trying times
your ability to laugh after an ashen day
your appreciative, funny remembering:
the student who placed an object in an unlikely orifice
or turned red when she saw you were listening, the one
whose work, materials are mysteriously lost in some sea
the flicked pencil, the girls wiggling in hilarious heels,
the pungency of that over dose of after shave. Please laugh,
keep laughing until your eyes water and belly breathes

I honor your strength
your presence shaping a class like an expert potter
the powerful look that can change the wrong channel
the clear, steely sound of your 'no,'
your calm abiding bringing comfort through tears
the way you can reach into that bottomless Poppins
bag and pull out exactly what's required to
save a lesson, steer a class, rectify any moment.
Your ability to engender love, true love, in those
young hearts that have so many beats left to take

No Child Left Behind, 2005

Dear President Bush:

I invite you to this school, challenge you
to find one child left behind. You will be tempted
to look only in the office file cabinets at scores…
come to the office, yes, but watch the secretaries
greet children in the morning, listen to the nurse
say "what's the matter dear" or come to the principal
to watch the way of loving discipline. Then walk to the gym
and see children enjoying exercise, listen for music flowing
from the stage, walk the halls and fill your senses with color,
stop in the library and read a book to a child. Keep walking,
peek in the classrooms to witness fathomless patience
step into any special education room and observe
unparalleled dedication. Look finally into the heart of
a teacher today, notice the joy for those who grow
more than hoped, mark the sorrow for those who do
not come further. You are a long way from the oval office
here, where lunch ladies, custodians, technicians,
teachers, social workers, consultants, counselors,
administrators, bus drivers, secretaries, nurses, parents
are tending to the needs of children daily.
Mr. President, it is not our school leaving the children behind.
Before your time, it was so; after your time, it will be so.
Rest easy sir: at this school all children accounted for--
safe, educated, appreciated.

The Master Teacher

Have you met our master teacher?
We like to pretend he is new this year
but he joins us every year in spring
and as a courtesy we smile, try to love him, tucking
our reluctance into the folds of our professionalism.
You know him, don't you? His name is Change.

He is an exacting master, we fear he is stern
he has no pencils, no paper, no plans
he has us open our books to pages unwritten,
we raise our hands though we do not know the answer
we line up continually but we do not know the way.
He offers one persistent direction: evolve.
Don't think Darwin, think you, me, us
we are all classmates, we will always be classmates in the
largest of classrooms sharing this same master teacher

Though at times we are tired and unmotivated
his direction compels us and his pointer prepares us
Look, there, a closed door   there, an open one
there a new job description   there a new grade,
there a new school   there a new class   there a new year
We must accept him as our teacher, he believes in us
sees our potential, our adaptability, our resilient strength.
Can we surrender to his evolutionary command, grow into
      this new me waiting for me
           this new you waiting for you
                this new us waiting for us?

A Single Star

A single point of light in darkness matters.
As the day exhales into dusk, so early now near solstice,
see that first star calling to you, holding you suspended in hope.
It promises to sustain you as our sun leaves us as it must,
poignantly sinking through thin bare trees

What are you hoping for, never-setting suns?
Then you forget we are miners drawn to descents into darkness
regularly misplacing the heartlamps graced to us when we howled
our way into this work at birth. Find a beam as the mountain
crumbles underfoot and light abandons the shaft, be cheered by
your capacity to save yourself and those around you from collapse

A new star once compelled three kings to follow and
inspired angels to sing a heartbreaking song of possible peace
to all humanity. The ones who had nothing heard then, the ones
looking in see now the quixotic promise visible at dusk:
a bowl of soup offered in illness, an unexpected laugh in labor,
a baby comforted by kindness after crying

Retiring Haiku

Spirit of the young:
open, playful, fresh and new
stay with me, always

www.ingramcontent.com/pod-product-compliance
Lightning Source LLC
Chambersburg PA
CBHW060224050426
42446CB00013B/3160